THE GRAMMAR
OF
CHINESE ORNAMENT

THE GRAMMAR

OF

CHINESE ORNAMENT

SELECTED FROM OBJECTS

IN THE

SOUTH KENSINGTON MUSEUM

AND OTHER COLLECTIONS.

BY

OWEN JONES.

ONE HUNDRED PLATES.

STUDIO EDITIONS
LONDON

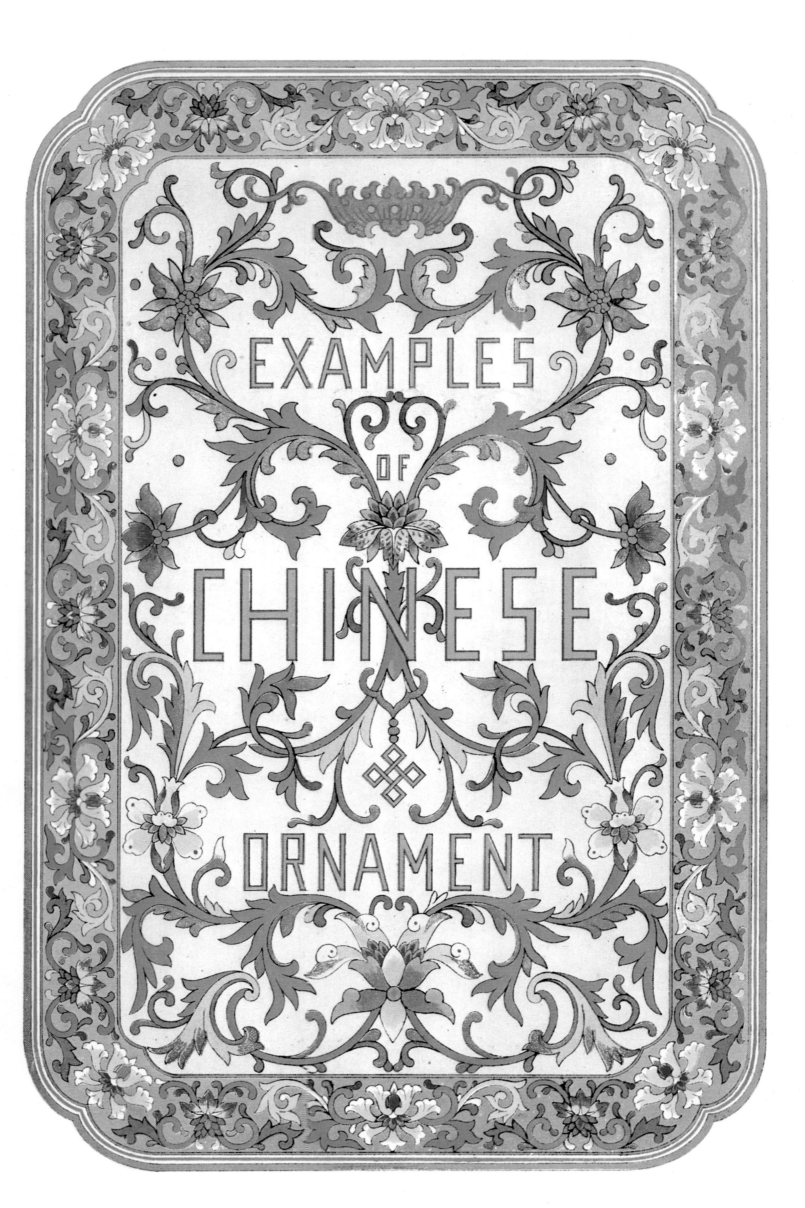

EXAMPLES

OF

CHINESE

ORNAMENT

Originally published by S. & T. Gilbert,
4 Copthall Buildings, London E.C. in 1867

This edition is published by Studio Editions,
a division of Bestseller Publications Ltd,
Princess House, 50 Eastcastle Street,
London W1N 7AP, England

Copyright © Studio Editions 1987

ISBN 1 85170 102 8

Printed and bound by Leefung-Asco Printers,
Hong Kong

OWEN JONES
1809 -1874

o/m

Owen Jones was the son of a famous Welsh antiquary. Trained as an architect and designer, he then became teacher of Applied Arts at the South Kensington School of Design. The first person to make a systematic study of Hispano-Moresque art and decoration, he travelled to the Middle East and Spain researching the original designs of these civilisations. Superintendent of Works for the Great Exhibition in London in 1851, he was in charge of the decoration for the Crystal Palace, and had a profound influence on the Arts and Crafts Movement of the nineteenth century, in particular on Morris and Ruskin.

His greatest published work was *The Grammar of Ornament,* which appeared in 1856. In it he collected an encyclopaedia of world ornament from early Egyptian and Greek patterns right through to the patterns of nature, so often found in the designs of William Morris. And today this remains one of the most sought-after and important source books for designers and illustrators.

Eleven years later Jones produced his second great work, *Examples of Chinese Ornament,* chronicling the patterns of Chinese ornament that were increasingly coming to the west as trade with China expanded. Originally published in a limited edition of 300 copies, this is one of the rarest books of the Victorian era and original copies are almost impossible to find. This Studio Editions reprint of that volume, now entitled *The Grammar of Chinese Ornament,* has been reproduced from one of the 300 original copies. As was common in those days, these plates were printed on stone and there was quite often a variation in the colour between the different copies. The reproduction in this volume has faithfully followed the original.

PREFACE.

THE late war in China, and the Ti-ping rebellion, by the destruction and sacking of many public buildings, has caused the introduction to Europe of a great number of truly magnificent works of Ornamental Art, of a character which had been rarely seen before that period, and which are remarkable, not only for the perfection and skill shown in the technical processes, but also for the beauty and harmony of the colouring, and general perfection of the ornamentation.

In the following Plates I have gathered together as great a variety of these new styles of Ornament as have come within my reach, and I trust that no important phase of this Art has escaped me.

I have had the advantage of access to the National Collection at South Kensington and the unrivalled collection of Alfred Morrison, Esq., of Fonthill, who has secured the finest specimens from time to time, as they have appeared in this country. From the collection of Louis Huth, Esq., exhibited in South Kensington, and from many objects in the possession of M. Digby Wyatt, Esq., Col. De La Rue, Thomas Chappell, Esq., F. O. Ward, Esq., Messrs. Nixon and Rhodes, and others, the bulk of the compositions have been obtained. My thanks are especially due to Messrs. Durlacher and Mr. Wareham for the liberal loan of many objects, which I have been thus enabled to copy in the quiet of the studio.

I venture to hope that the publication of these types of a style of Ornament hitherto little known will be found, by all those in the practice of Ornamental Art, a valuable and instructive aid in building up what we all seek,—the progressive development of the forms of the past, founded on the eternal principles which all good forms of Art display.

OWEN JONES.

9 Argyll Place,
    July 15, 1867.

CHINESE ORNAMENT.

WE have long been familiar with the power of the Chinese to balance colours, but we were not so well acquainted with their power of treating purely ornamental or conventional forms ; and in the chapter in the *Grammar of Ornament* on Chinese Ornament I was led, from my then knowledge, to express the opinion that the Chinese had not the power of dealing with conventional ornamental form : but it now appears that there has been a period in which a School of Art existed in China of a very important kind. We are led to think that this art must in some way have had a foreign origin ; it so nearly resembles in all its principles the art of the Mohammedan races, that we may presume it was derived from them. It would be no difficult task to take a work of ornament of this class, and, by simply varying the colouring and correcting the drawing, convert it into an Indian or Persian composition. There is of course, in all these works, something essentially Chinese in the mode of rendering the idea, but the original idea is evidently Mohammedan.

The Moors of the present day decorate their pottery under the same instinct, and follow the same laws as the Chinese obeyed in their beautiful enamelled vases. The Moorish artist takes a rudely-fashioned pot or other object, and by a marvellous instinct divides the surface of the object, by spots of colour, into triangles of proportionate area, according to the form and size of the object ; these triangles are then crossed by others,

Ornament from a Moorish Jar.

formed with spots of a different colour. All these spots are then united by a continuous line, suggested by the peculiar form they have taken on the surface of the object. The spaces thus created are filled in with other spots and lines, in the direction of, or in contrast to, the leading lines, and are then still further filled up by smaller spots, till the whole presents an even tint or bloom.

The Chinese in the works now under review must have proceeded in the same way. The position of the larger flowers was first fixed in the position most suited to develope the peculiar form of the vase, and the whole surface was set out by these flowers into symmetrical proportional areas ; here law and order were abandoned, and the instinct and caprice of the artist came into play, in uniting all these fixed centres by a flowing line. This flowing line then dividing the different triangular spaces irregularly, masses of intermediate size, either as flowers or large leaves, were put in, springing from the continuous line ; these secondary masses also balance triangularly, but in a less rigid manner than with the larger flowers : the process is continued by the introduction within the intermediate spaces of still smaller forms, buds, or stalks, till the whole is filled up, and repose is obtained by evenness of tint. This method of composition is followed in all the Oriental styles of ornament : what is peculiar to the Chinese, especially in their large enamelled objects, is the large relative size of the principal flowers which mark the triangulation of the areas ; and it will be seen throughout the plates how cleverly this apparent disproportion of the principal points of the composition is got over by the detail on the surface of the flower, so that the desirable evenness of tint is preserved.

This method of having fixed symmetrically arranged spots, round which run leaves and branches, was characteristic of Roman Ornament, which generally consisted of a scroll growing out of another scroll encircling a flower.

Roman Ornament.

The bulb at the point of junction of the volutes was got rid of during the Byzantine period ; and in the Arabian and Moresque, and Oriental styles generally, the end of the scroll becomes flattened out into the form of a leaf; the flowers flow off the continuous stem. In the Renaissance style the peculiarity of Roman Ornament reappeared, but much more sparingly as other elements were introduced : it was subordinate, but still ever present ; every volute is terminated by a flower. In the Persian, which comes much

6

nearer our present style, the flowers are placed, not at the end of a volute, but at the junction of two tangential curves; so in the Indian style : in neither of these styles is the system of triangulation so rigidly carried out : it is always the guiding principle, but it is more artistically concealed. In the Chinese ornamentation, triangulation is the main feature, the geometrical arrangement is absolute and undisguised, but softened by a free treatment of the intermediate spaces left by the triangulation.

An examination of the plates will satisfactorily prove, that in the style under discussion the principles advocated in the *Grammar of Ornament*, as derived from natural laws, and found in all the Oriental styles, are here also universally obeyed.

We say by Proposition 10 of the *Grammar of Ornament :*

> " Harmony of form consists in the proper balancing and contrast of the straight, the inclined, and the curved."

By Proposition 11 :

> " In surface decoration all lines should flow out of a parent stem. Every ornament, however distant, should be traced to its branch and root."

By Proposition 12 :

> " All junctions of curved lines with curved, or of curved lines with straight, should be tangential with each other.'

By Proposition 13 :

> " Flowers, or other natural objects, should not be used as ornaments; but conventional representations founded upon them, sufficiently suggestive to convey the intended image to the mind, without destroying the unity of the object they are employed to decorate."

We shall find that in this style Proposition 10 is most completely obeyed.

Proposition 11 also, with this proviso; that we have two well-marked styles ; one entirely in accordance with Proposition 11, and the other where, in the same composition, there are several centres : but in all cases the leaves and flowers can be traced to their branch and root, though in what we have ventured to call the fragmentary style there are many roots in the same composition.

Proposition 12 also here finds its full exemplification. In some of the enamelled work there is a stiffness at the point of junction of two curves, but it is always the result of imperfect execution. The intention always is to make them tangential.

The examples are not so apparently in accordance with Proposition 13. We think in this style the Chinese have reached the extreme limit of the representation of natural objects. They have, however, in none of our examples, by light or shade, endeavoured to express relief, though in many of the examples it is suggested both by colour and form ; indeed, we think that the chief value of the publication of this style of ornament lies in its suggestive character : it shows how unnecessary it is to be content with the stock forms ; and that many natural objects may be conventionally rendered in ornamentation without overstepping the bounds of propriety. We repeat, however, that the

7

Chinese have in this style reached the very limit of such possible representations, and that a more moderate suggestion of relief would be more artistic.

The compositions will be found to range under the three systems represented in the diagrams.

1. The Continuous-stem System.

2. The Fragmentary System united.

3. The Fragmentary System interspacing.

The scheme of colouring of the Chinese is peculiarly their own. They deal principally with broken colours: pale blue, pale green, and pale pink for the masses; dark pink, dark green, purple, and yellow and white, in much smaller quantities. There is nothing crude or harsh in any of their compositions; the eye is perfectly satisfied with the balance and arrangement of both form and colour; but there is an absence of that purity in the drawing which we find in the works of the ancient Greeks, Arabs, and Moors, and even in the works of our own day, of all the Mahommedan races.

8

DESCRIPTION OF THE PLATES.

PLATE I.

Ornamental Title, arranged from a painted china dish.

PLATE II.

This plate is taken from a very fine Vase of blue-and-white china. The large flowers are arranged all over the surface of the Vase in equilateral triangles, and are united by one continuous main stem, throwing off smaller masses arranged triangularly. The introduction of the ground colour in the centre of the flowers is very valuable, and materially helps the repose of the composition.

PLATE III.

This plate is arranged from a blue-and-white china Basin, and shows half the circumference of the basin developed. The four pear-shaped masses are very effective. The etched outline flowers on the dark ground are after the Indian manner; so also is the general arrangement of the pendant ornament, except that the scrolls have their terminations so peculiarly Chinese.

PLATE IV.

This plate is taken from a large Vase, similar in general arrangement to that from which Plate II. is taken, but the forms of the Ornament are much less pure. The composition consists of three bats placed triangularly, crossed by three flowers similarly arranged in the opposite direction: these are all united by a continuous stem, throwing off other masses of conventional form.

PLATE V.

A similar composition on a dark ground. Here repose is obtained by the etching in the ground-colour, on the leaves and flowers.

PLATE VI.

Part of a pendant Ornament round the top of a magnificent blue-and-white china cistern. In the upper border the lines run in one direction round the bowl. In the lower, one continuous main stem runs through the general forms, embracing all the flowers, which are geometrically arranged. The broad blue line which forms the boundary of the composition is also continuous; and in the form of a pendant arch recalls a form which is common to the Arabian, Persian, Moresque, and indeed all Oriental art. The treatment of the shading of the flowers is also Indian in character.

PLATE VII.

From a blue-and-white china Dish. Again in this example we see a Persian influence in the flowers round the edge, and in the form of the external rim of the dish.

PLATE VIII.

From a blue-and-white china Bottle. Here we have continuous stems running round the bottle, throwing off flowers right and left, fitting into each other as it were, and yet triangulation is never lost sight of.

PLATE IX.

Borders from blue-and-white china Bottles.

PLATE X.

Borders from Vases in cloisonné enamel. The same instinct of triangulation may be observed in the colouring of the ornament.

X

PLATE XI.

The same principles which are exhibited in Plate II. are to be seen in this specimen from a Bowl in cloisonné enamel. The large flowers are arranged in triangles, crossed by smaller flowers in the opposite direction, and all connected by a continuous stem throwing off leaves and stalks to fill up the ground; all geometrically arranged, and yet not in a manner so apparent as to interfere with the freedom of the composition. The system of triangulation is still further kept up in the colouring. On the left the purple flower is the apex of a triangle, with two red flowers for a base (the left one not being contained on the plate). In the same way, on the right of the plate, the light-green flower is the apex of a triangle, with two dark-green flowers at the base. The white flower is the centre of the composition, and stands alone, and yet its centre lies between two small red flowers which form the base of a triangle having a green flower for the apex.

XI

PLATE XII.

Portion of the circumference of a large Bowl in cloisonné enamel. This composition is repeated twice round the bowl, and the lines all spring from the centre flower. Although not on the formal principle of the composition last described, the same system of triangulation of form and colour is apparent at a glance.

PLATE XIII.

From an Incense-burner in cloisonné enamel. The flowers are arranged over the surface in equilateral triangles, and are crossed by stems with volute terminations, also triangular, but less formal, which fill up the interstices.

PLATE XIV.

This plate represents half the circumference of a Vase in cloisonné enamel. The arrangement of form and colour is most artistic.

PLATE XV.

From a cloisonné-enamelled Bowl. This composition is similar in principle to that of Plate XI., but the large flowers are more perfect in form and detail.

PLATE XVI.

Borders from similar Vases.

PLATE XVII.

This singular composition is from the handle of a Standard in cloisonné enamel, the black ground represents the portion which is pierced (à jour). A main stem winds round the staff, through the large flowers, which are, as usual, triangularly placed.

PLATE XVIII.

From a painted china Bottle. The general form of this border, like that on Plate VI., has a very Indian outline. The flowers here are also com-

posed triangularly, and are all united by one main stem, which runs round the circumference of the Bottle.

PLATE XIX.

From a china Dish, the pattern being stamped or engraved on the clay before colouring. This is a specimen of a style of ornament of which there are to be found immense varieties. It is probably much more modern than the specimens already described. We have still the instinct of triangular composition, but it is not so decidedly marked; the centre flower occupies more relative space, and the stems out of which the flowers spring, instead of flowing onwards in a series of volutes, often re-enter and return upon themselves. This principle is essentially Chinese, whilst the flowing line is common to the Arabian, Moresque, Persian, and Indian styles. The border on the edge of the dish is almost Greek.

PLATE XX.

The same observations will apply to this plate, which is taken from a painted china Dish. Although all the groups are united, they do not, as in the finer examples we have examined, proceed from one centre. In this example, also, the pattern is indented, showing that probably some mechanical means were employed to produce it; whilst on such Vases as Plates II., III., and V., they were freely drawn by the hand without any mechanical aid.

PLATE XXI.

A series of Borders from various objects, in blue and white china.

PLATE XXII.

Centre of a Plate and various Diapers, from objects in blue and white china. The border on the upper portion of the plate is an interesting example of the conventional representation of natural flowers symmetrically arranged; after the Persian manner.

PLATE XXIII.

From a Bottle of blue and white china; a very fine example of symmetrical arrangement: it is also interesting as showing the limit of shade and relief in the representation of flowers—a limit which the Chinese constantly reach, but never exceed.

PLATE XXIV.

From a blue-and-white china Cistern. This is a noble composition, on the same principle as those already described. The artistic introduction of the white lines on the dark ground, and the outline to flowers and leaves on the white ground, so as in each case to soften the transition, is worthy of remark.

PLATE XXV.

From objects in blue-and-white china.

PLATE XXVI.

From a blue-and-white china Bottle. This composition, like that of Plate XXIII., is a fine example of the conventional representation of natural flowers; but for the peculiar character of the termination of some of the leaves, it would pass for Indian or Persian.

PLATE XXVII.

From various objects in blue-and-white china. The centre composition and the borders at the top of the plate are very Persian in character and arrangement.

PLATE XXVIII.

From a blue-and-white china Bottle. This composition is peculiar, but not inelegant; notwithstanding the fragmentary nature of the composition the masses are well balanced, and the repose of the whole is not destroyed.

PLATE XXIX.

The inside and outside of a very finely executed Bowl in cloisonné enamel. On the inside of the bowl we have a conventional representation of the land, the sea, and the air. The land by the flower on the island, the sea by the horses disporting themselves in the waves, and the air by bats and birds floating in clouds.

XXIX

PLATE XXX.

From a very beautifully executed Basin in cloisonné enamel.

PLATE XXXI.

From Vases in cloisonné enamel.

PLATE XXXII.

From a square Vase in cloisonné enamel. The outline of this vase is very elegant, and the composition of the ornament contrasting with the curved lines is very fine. The pattern on the lower half of the plate is from the inside of the lip.

PLATE XXXIII.

From a similar Vase, but less perfectly executed. The filling up of the side of the vase is very fine in composition. The pattern on the inside of the lip is less perfect than that on the last plate.

PLATE XXXIV.

From a similar Vase, but of the round form. The upper portion of the plate is from the inside of the lip.

PLATE XXXV.

From a Bowl in cloisonné enamel. In the centre pattern we have a fine example of continuity of leading stem.

PLATE XXXVI.

From a large Jar in cloisonné enamel. The style of this composition is essentially Chinese; though very brilliant in colouring, it is much less perfect in art than the compositions in which we recognise a foreign influence.

PLATE XXXVII.

From a Bowl in cloisonné enamel. This composition, like the last, is entirely Chinese in character.

PLATE XXXVIII.

From a Dish in cloisonné enamel. This also is essentially Chinese in character. Four bats with outspread wings, and connected at their extremities, make up the composition: in the centre is a kind of labyrinth.

PLATE XXXIX.

Fragments from cloisonné-enamelled Vases, showing various applications of the fret patterns.

PLATE XL.

From Vases in cloisonné enamel. The upper border is composed of bats with outspread wings. The pattern on the lower half of the sheet does not appear to be based on any principle, yet evenness of tint is very cleverly obtained.

PLATE XLI.

From a very beautiful painted china Bottle; but for the peculiar Chinese twist to the leaves and scrolls it might pass for Indian lacquer-work.

PLATE XLII.

Also from a painted china Bottle. This composition, unlike the last, is essentially Chinese; not only the flowers and leaves have the peculiar Chinese character, but the fragmentary style of the composition, starting from the flowers, yet linked together, is much less artistic than the continuous stem seeking out and embracing all the flowers symmetrically arranged.

PLATE XLIII.

From a gourd-shaped painted china Vase. We have here an example of the continuous-stem principle referred to in the last plate.

PLATE XLIV.

From a painted china Bottle. This again is a specimen of what we have ventured to call fragmentary style. The same principle of triangulation is observed in this style, and the patterns springing from different centres fit into each other in a marvellous manner, so that the repose of the whole is not disturbed.

PLATE XLV.

On this sheet we have juxtaposed specimens of the two styles; the upper border on the continuous line principle, and the lower border on the detached or fragmentary style.

PLATE XLVI.

From a very elegant painted china Vase. The red flowers are spread all over the vase, in as near as may be equilateral triangles, and they are all united by the continuous stem, which winds spirally round the vase.

PLATE XLVII.

From a painted china Vase, in the same style and on the same principle as the various compositions in cloisonné enamel before described.

PLATE XLVIII.

From a painted china Bottle. We recognise here a mixed style; the flowing stem and treatment of the flowers is after the Persian and Indian manner, whilst the form of the leaves is exactly that used in what we have called the fragmentary style.

PLATE XLIX.

From a copper Dish in the form of a shell; surface enamel. This composition is also in the mixed style. On the radiating lines the flowers and ornaments are detached. In the intermediate spaces one continuous stem starting from the base embraces all the flowers. In the drawing of the flowers, also, we see evidences of this mixed style: some of the flowers are Chinese in character, whilst others are drawn in the Persian and Indian manner.

12

PLATE L.

From a very beautiful painted Vase. Again we have this mixed style in a very marked manner; the composition is of the detached character, starting from many centres, yet all linked together. Some of the flowers are treated quite conventionally, whilst others have a much nearer approach to nature. The light-running ground pattern, which is indented on the vase before painting, is continuous all over the vase.

PLATE LI.

From a painted china Vase. Although on the fragmentary principle, the composition on this vase is very elegant; both forms and colours are beautifully arranged and balanced.

PLATE LII.

Various compositions on the fragmentary principle. The upper pattern on the left is from cloisonné enamel, the other from painted china vases.

PLATE LIII.

From an elegant Bottle, surface enamel on copper. We have here a natural treatment of flowers, in which the limit of flat treatment may be said to have been reached. The principle of composition is essentially Persian, though the scheme of colouring could only be Chinese. The elegant border in the centre of the plate marks the neck of the bottle where the swell of the lower half commences.

PLATE LIV.

Compositions in similar style to those of the last plate, but from painted china basins.

PLATE LV.

From a surface-enamelled copper Bottle. The upper border with the dragons forms the neck of the bottle, and is on the fragmentary principle. The lower part of the bottle is on the continuous-stem principle.

PLATE LVI.

From a painted china Bottle. In this composition the dragon-flies are arranged triangularly, and crossed by the large flowers similarly arranged.

PLATE LVII.

From a surface-enamelled copper Bottle. This composition is in the fragmentary style, though very well filled up.

PLATE LVIII.

From a painted china Jar. This is a fine example of the detached style, and is, in the treatment of both leaves and flowers, essentially Chinese.

PLATE LIX.

From a surface-enamelled copper Bottle. In the principal border on this plate we have a further example of fragmentary composition, so well arranged that the patterns fit into each other, and appear continuous. The border below, composed of frets, is singularly like the same treatment of the fret on the monuments of Central America. The attempt to represent the human face will be readily recognised.

PLATE LX.

From a very elegant painted china Dish.

PLATE LXI.

From objects in cloisonné enamel. The centre specimen on this plate is a very charming example of continuous line in composition, and is most artistic in the management of the colours. The three red centres of the flowers accentuate the triangle; the green of the centre flower is recalled on the white flower, and the dark purple also on the flower on the left. So also the white of the right-hand flower is carried over on the left; the green bud at the base, recalling the green mass at the top, is also excessively valuable, as giving perpendicularity to the composition. It is difficult to imagine a more exquisite instance of order enlivened by caprice, than in the present example.

The border on the lower portion of the plate is one of those odd compositions so constantly met with, and which would appear to have a meaning, but which is difficult for the European mind to seize. The centre portion is evidently intended to represent a face; the eyes, nose, and mouth can be deciphered.

LXI

PLATE LXII.

From a most exquisitely painted china Bottle. Although painted china, this is evidently in the same style and of the same period as the bulk of the cloisonné enamels, the gold outline circling the colours having the same harmonizing office as on the enamelled vases. The very stiffness of line consequent on the process is here unnecessarily imitated in the painting, where a freer treatment was at command. For balance of form and colour, and for pure conventional treatment, this is one of the finest specimens we have met with.

LXII

PLATE LXIII.

From various objects in cloisonné enamel. The fragment at the top of the plate is from the rim of a large dish, the black representing the part which is pierced. The circular pattern is from a plate, the different spaces are very admirably filled up. The lower specimen is of a style of which there are many examples, both in enamelled objects and painted china. It may be said to be a style without principle of any kind; the flowers are thrown about on the ground as at hap-hazard, one set of triangles behind another, and yet they are generally so well distributed that a pleasing effect is produced: an effect, however, which cannot procure that permanent pleasure which we derive from studying a composition formed in obedience to law.

LXIII

PLATE LXIV.

From various objects in cloisonné enamel. The centre composition on the plate is one of the most elegant of the fragmentary class, and is essentially Chinese in character. The lower border, formed by ornamental dragons, is remarkable for the way in which the nondescript animals fill up the space in which they float.

PLATE LXV.

Another example from a painted china Bottle, of pure Chinese composition.

PLATE LXVI.

From a painted china Bottle. Similar in character to the last plate.

PLATE LXVII.

Another of the same class, painted china.

PLATE LXVIII.

From a painted china Bottle. The upper portion of the plate is from the neck of the bottle, the lower portion is chiefly remarkable for the clever way in which the white of the large flower is distributed over the remainder of the space.

PLATE LXIX.

From a painted china Vase. A very fine example of triangulation and the continuous - stem principle.

PLATE LXX.

From a painted china Bottle, similar to that described on Plate XLVI., but much bolder in treatment.

PLATE LXXI.

From a painted china Jar. The principle of composition on this bottle is the same as on Plates LXX. and XLVI., only the continuous line runs horizontally instead of spirally round the bottle, and the repeat is moved one-half a division, so as to bring the flowers into triangles. To compose a pattern which shall do this, and thoroughly and evenly fill up the space, is not easy, and is only attained by the Oriental instinct.

PLATE LXXII.

Portions of the painted china Jar described on the last plate; the ornament in the centre of the plate is from the lid of the jar.

PLATE LXXIII.

From painted china Vases. The upper border on this plate is a curious specimen of a continuous stem running round the vase, and throwing off a light and a dark flower side-by-side; in the centre of each flower is the Chinese emblem of the labyrinth.

PLATE LXXIV.

From a painted china Bottle. In the upper border, which is from the neck of the bottle, the different patterns are united; but in the lower pattern, from the swell of the bottle, the compositions are entirely fragmentary, and yet so contrived that the ornament is very evenly distributed over the ground.

PLATE LXXV.

From a painted china Bottle. This composition is in the mixed style. The main stems are continuous, and embrace all the flowers; but there are distributed over the surface detached emblems, unconnected with the composition.

PLATE LXXVI.

From a painted china Vase. A composition on the continuous-stem principle.

PLATE LXXVII.

From a painted china Bottle. A composition in the fragmentary style. Pure Chinese in character.

PLATE LXXVIII.

From a painted china Bottle. This composition is so completely after the Persian and Indian manner, that it would require no other change than to be coloured after the Indian or Persian scheme of colouring to be an Indian or Persian work.

14

PLATE LXXIX.

From a painted china Bottle. This composition is very interesting. One main stem winds round the base of the bottle, throwing up stems and branches fitting into the shape to the top of the bottle, where a change of colour of the ground only, accentuates the neck of the bottle. In colour, form and line, it is entirely Chinese.

PLATE LXXX.

From a painted china Bottle. The observations we have made on Plate LXXVIII. apply equally to this composition. It is Indian in form and line, and is Chinese only in its colouring.

PLATE LXXXI.

From a very large Cistern in cloisonné enamel. This magnificent composition is in every way Chinese, and is the very perfection of conventional ornamentation, perfect in distribution of form and colour.

PLATE LXXXII.

From a painted china Vase. A very fine example of detached or fragmentary ornamentation.

PLATE LXXXIII.

From a painted china Vase. Similar style to the last, but more perfect; in the balance of the masses, the embossed ground is formed of a continuous line of volutes.

PLATE LXXXIV.

From a painted china Vase. This style is still more fragmentary: the compositions are entirely detached in its general effect; it is yet very elegant. As before, the embossed ground is continuous.

PLATE LXXXV.

From painted china. The upper example is from a Basin; the lower is from a portion of a Vase.

PLATE LXXXVI.

Portion of a painted china Dish: four dragons guarding the labyrinth form the subject of the composition, the flowers are most artistically arranged in the fragmentary style.

PLATE LXXXVII.

From a painted china Bottle. This is another of those compositions such as are described on Plates LXXX. and LXXVIII., which are Chinese only from their scheme of colouring.

PLATE LXXXVIII.

From painted china. The upper composition is of the same Indian character as the last plate; the little dish in the form of a star has very much the same character. The geometric arrangement of the groups of flowers, without being rigidly accurate, yet sufficiently so to properly balance, is most artistic.

PLATE LXXXIX.

From a large painted china Cistern. This composition is thoroughly Indian, like Plates LXXVIII., LXXX., and LXXXVII.

PLATE XC.

From a painted china Vase. A bold composition in the Indian manner.

PLATE XCI.

From painted china. The upper subject from a small Tray, is remarkable for the way in which the flowers fill up the space.

PLATE XCII.

From a painted china Vase. A bold composition on the continuous-stem principle.

PLATE XCIII.

From a painted china Bottle. There is much of the Indian character in this example, particularly in the detached flowers at the base of the subject.

PLATE XCIV.

From a painted china Jar. Composition on the fragmentary principle; remarkable for the bold treatment of the top and bottom of the jar.

PLATE XCV.

From a painted china Vase. Another composition on the fragmentary principle.

PLATE XCVI.

From a painted china Bottle. A singular composition; remarkable for the way in which the effect of the strong colour of the ornament is softened by the judicious treatment of the ground.

PLATE XCVII.

From a painted china Bottle. Composition on the continuous-stem principle. The ornament in this example is in slight relief. The vase was cast in a mould.

PLATE XCVIII.

Inlaid bronze Dish.

PLATE XCIX.

From a painted china Bottle. Composition on the continuous-stem principle.

PLATE C.

From a painted china Vase. This example can hardly be called ornament: it is conventional only in the way in which the leaves and fruit are balanced.

Ornament from an Indian Lacquer Box.

15

THE PLATES

PLATE II.

This plate is taken from a very fine Vase of blue-and-white china. The large flowers are arranged all over the surface of the Vase in equilateral triangles, and are united by one continuous main stem, throwing off smaller masses arranged triangularly. The introduction of the ground colour in the centre of the flowers is very valuable, and materially helps the repose of the composition.

PLATE III.

This plate is arranged from a blue-and-white china Basin, and shows half the circumference of the basin developed. The four pear-shaped masses are very effective. The etched outline flowers on the dark ground are after the Indian manner; so also is the general arrangement of the pendant ornament, except that the scrolls have their terminations so peculiarly Chinese.

PLATE IV.

This plate is taken from a large Vase, similar in general arrangement to that from which Plate II. is taken, but the forms of the Ornament are much less pure. The composition consists of three bats placed triangularly, crossed by three flowers similarly arranged in the opposite direction: these are all united by a continuous stem, throwing off other masses of conventional form.

Plate VI.

Part of a pendant Ornament round the top of a magnificent blue-and-white china cistern. In the upper border the lines run in one direction round the bowl. In the lower, one continuous main stem runs through the general forms, embracing all the flowers, which are geometrically arranged. The broad blue line which forms the boundary of the composition is also continuous; and in the form of a pendant arch recalls a form which is common to the Arabian, Persian, Moresque, and indeed all Oriental art. The treatment of the shading of the flowers is also Indian in character.

PLATE VII.

From a blue-and-white china Dish. Again in this example we see a Persian influence in the flowers round the edge, and in the form of the external rim of the dish.

PLATE IX.

Borders from blue-and-white china Bottles.

PLATE XI.

The same principles which are exhibited in Plate II. are to be seen in this specimen from a Bowl in cloisonné enamel. The large flowers are arranged in triangles, crossed by smaller flowers in the opposite direction, and all connected by a continuous stem throwing off leaves and stalks to fill up the ground ; all geometrically arranged, and yet not in a manner so apparent as to interfere with the freedom of the composition. The system of triangulation is still further kept up in the colouring. On the left the purple flower is the apex of a triangle, with two red flowers for a base (the left one not being contained on the plate). In the same way, on the right of the plate, the light-green flower is the apex of a triangle, with two dark-green flowers at the base. The white flower is the centre of the composition, and stands alone, and yet its centre lies between two small red flowers which form the base of a triangle having a green flower for the apex.

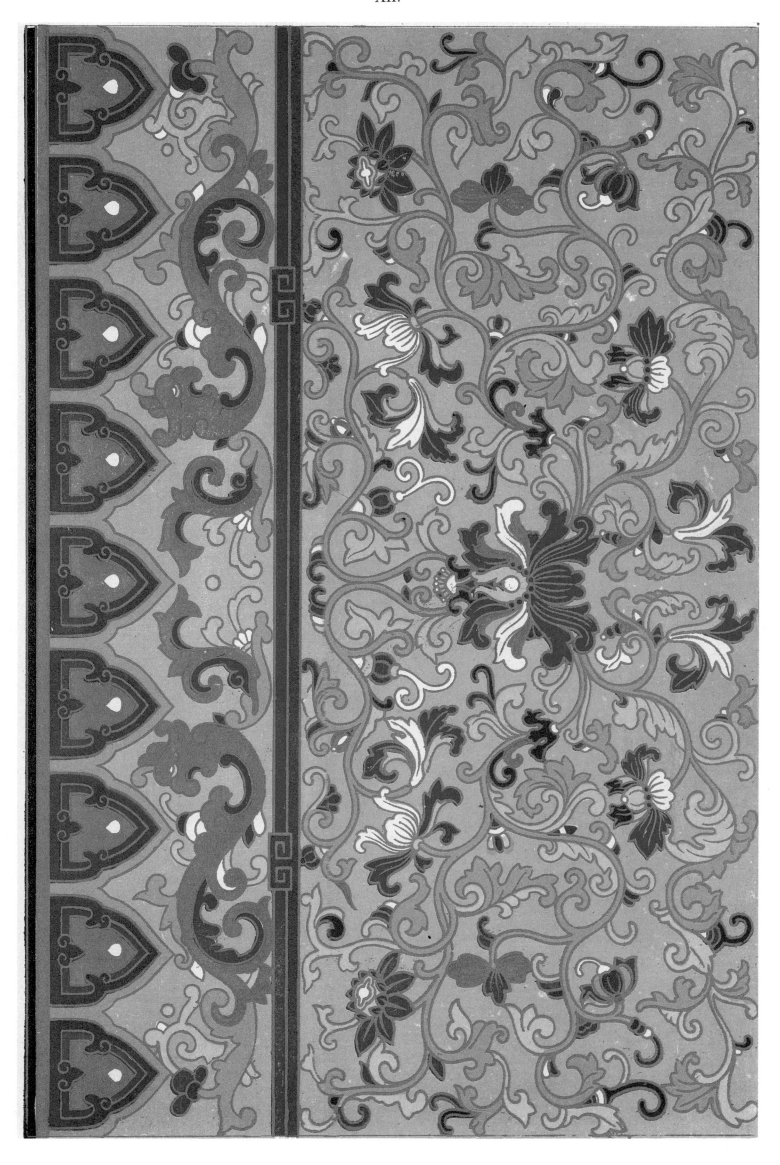

PLATE XVI.

Borders from similar Vases.

PLATE XVII.

This singular composition is from the handle of a Standard in cloisonné enamel, the black ground represents the portion which is pierced (*à jour*). A main stem winds round the staff, through the large flowers, which are, as usual, triangularly placed.

From a painted china Bottle. The general
form of this border, like that on Plate VI., has a
very Indian outline. The flowers here are also composed triangularly, and are all united by one main
stem, which runs round the circumference of the
Bottle.

PLATE XIX.

From a china Dish, the pattern being stamped
or engraved on the clay before colouring. This is a
specimen of a style of ornament of which there are
to be found immense varieties. It is probably much
more modern than the specimens already described.
We have still the instinct of triangular composition,
but it is not so decidedly marked; the centre flower
occupies more relative space, and the stems out of
which the flowers spring, instead of flowing onwards
in a series of volutes, often re-enter and return upon
themselves. This principle is essentially Chinese,
whilst the flowing line is common to the Arabian,
Moresque, Persian, and Indian styles. The border
on the edge of the dish is almost Greek.

PLATE XX.

The same observations will apply to this plate,
which is taken from a painted china Dish. Although all the groups are united, they do not, as in
the finer examples we have examined, proceed from
one centre. In this example, also, the pattern is
indented, showing that probably some mechanical
means were employed to produce it; whilst on such
Vases as Plates II., III., and V., they were freely
drawn by the hand without any mechanical aid.

PLATE XXI.

A series of Borders from various objects, in blue and white china.

XXII.

Plate XXIV.

From a blue-and-white china Cistern. This is a
noble composition, on the same principle as those
already described. The artistic introduction of the
white lines on the dark ground, and the outline to
flowers and leaves on the white ground, so as in
each case to soften the transition, is worthy of
remark.

Plate **XXXII**.

From a square Vase in cloisonné enamel. The outline of this vase is very elegant, and the composition of the ornament contrasting with the curved lines is very fine. The pattern on the lower half of the plate is from the inside of the lip.

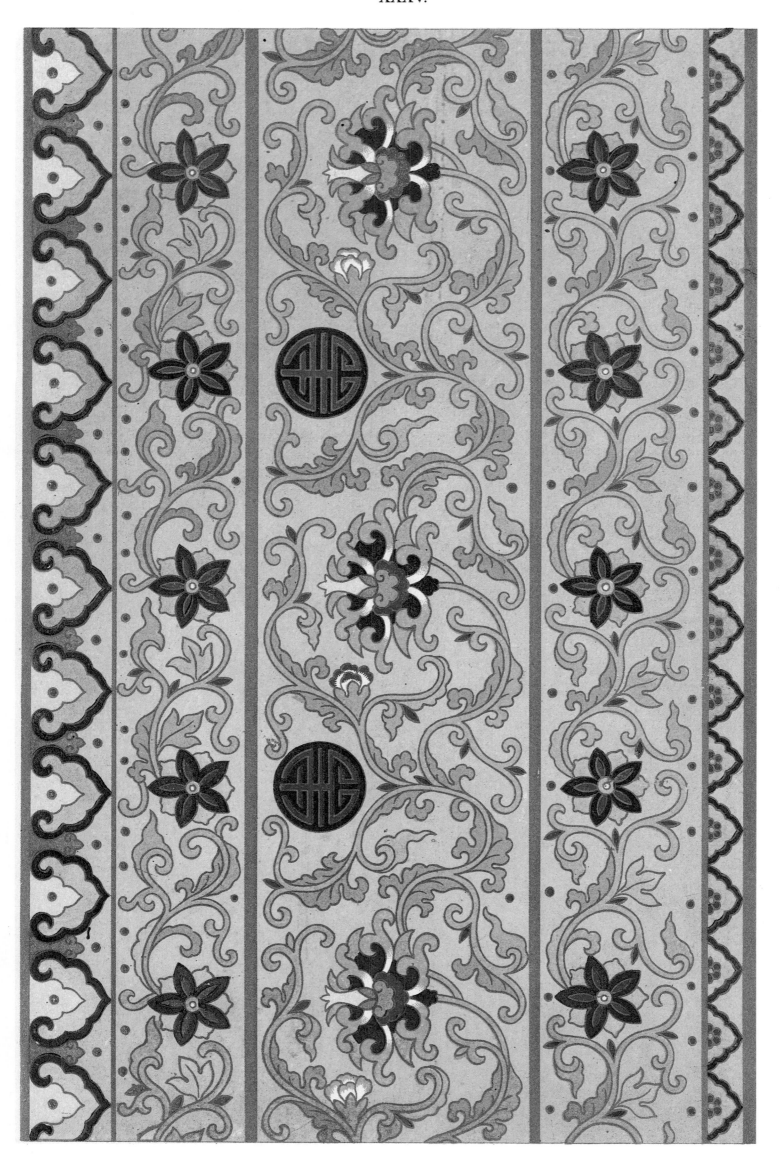

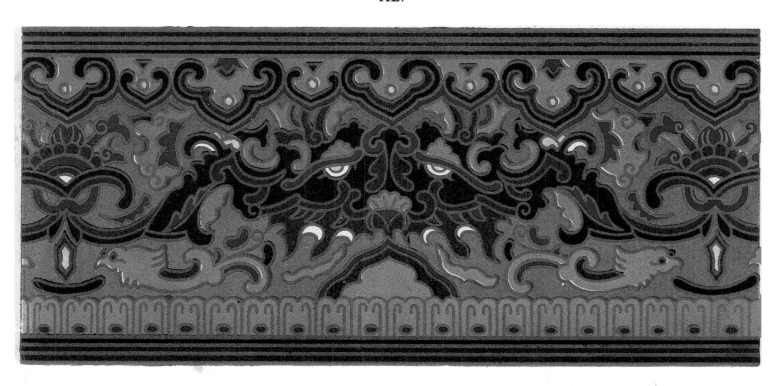

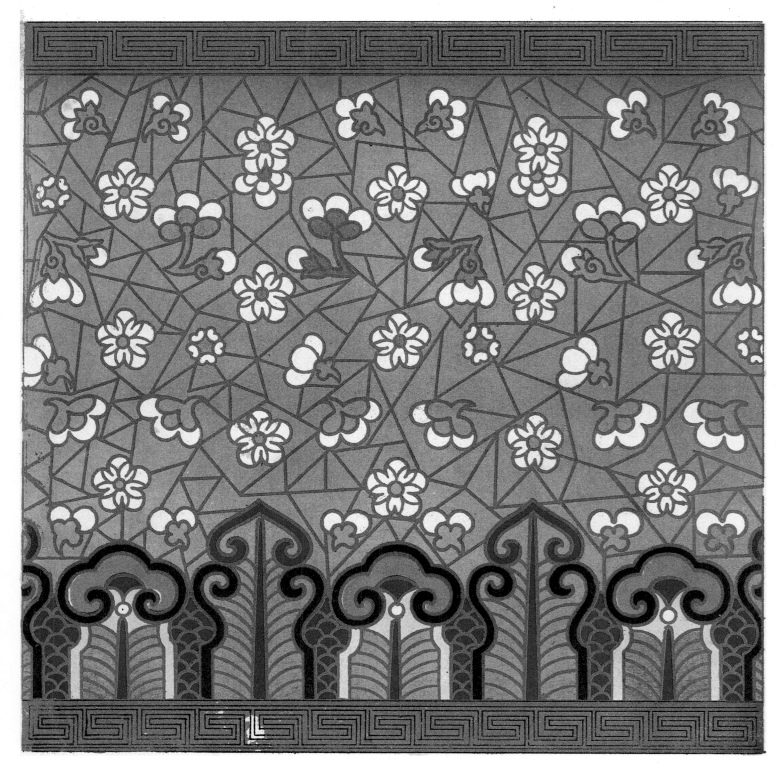

PLATE XLII.

Also from a painted china Bottle. This composition, unlike the last, is essentially Chinese; not only the flowers and leaves have the peculiar Chinese character, but the fragmentary style of the composition, starting from the flowers, yet linked together, is much less artistic than the continuous stem seeking out and embracing all the flowers symmetrically arranged.

PLATE XLIII.

From a gourd-shaped painted china Vase. We have here an example of the continuous-stem principle referred to in the last plate.

Plate XLIV.

From a painted china Bottle. This again is a specimen of what we have ventured to call fragmentary style. The same principle of triangulation is observed in this style, and the patterns springing from different centres fit into each other in a marvellous manner, so that the repose of the whole is not disturbed.

Plate XLV.

On this sheet we have juxtaposed specimens of the two styles ; the upper border on the continuous line principle, and the lower border on the detached or fragmentary style.

Plate XLIX.

From a copper Dish in the form of a shell; surface enamel. This composition is also in the mixed style. On the radiating lines the flowers and ornaments are detached. In the intermediate spaces one continuous stem starting from the base embraces all the flowers. In the drawing of the flowers, also, we see evidences of this mixed style: some of the flowers are Chinese in character, whilst others are drawn in the Persian and Indian manner.

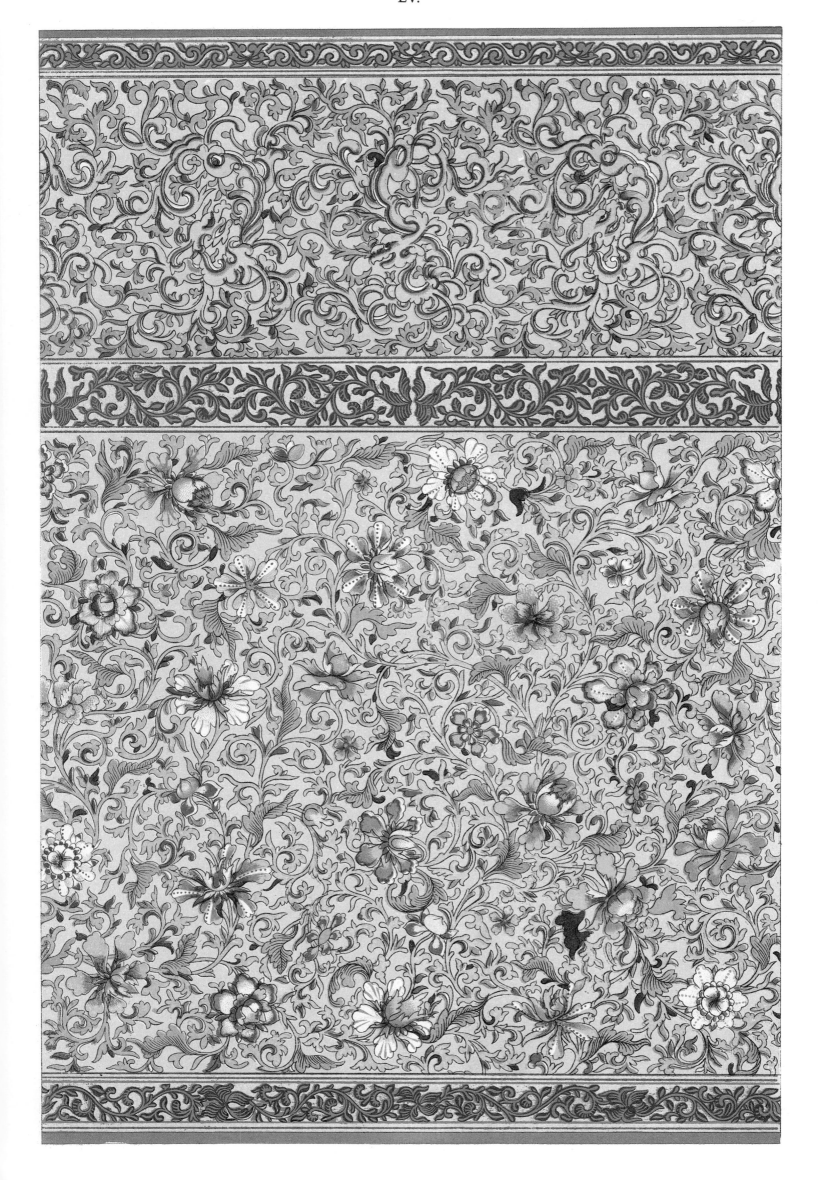

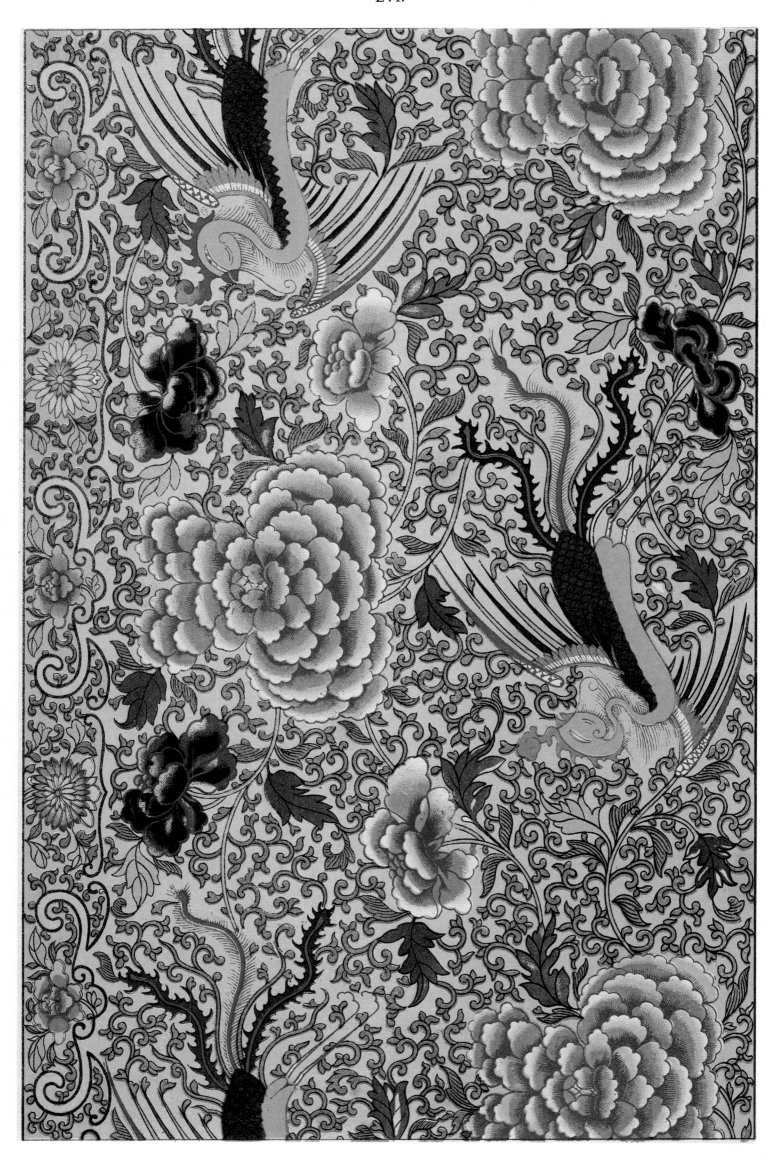

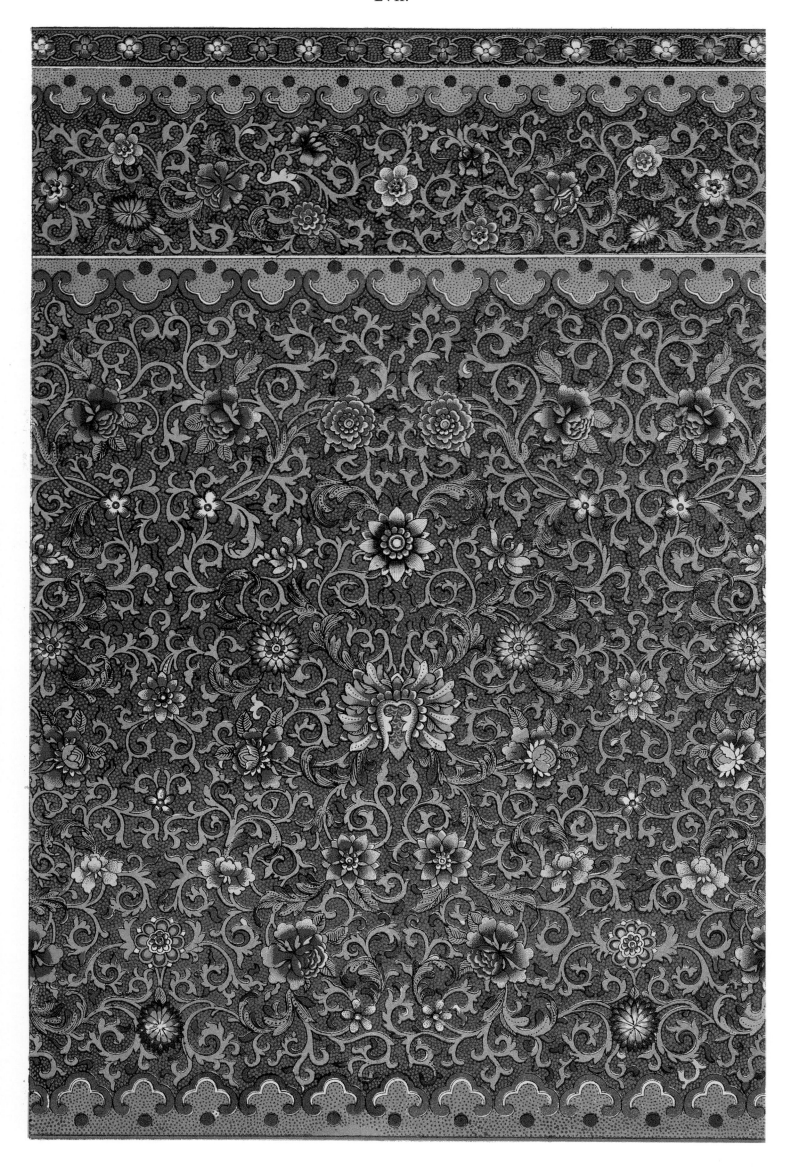

Plate LXI.

From objects in cloisonné enamel. The centre specimen on this plate is a very charming example of continuous line in composition, and is most artistic in the management of the colours. The three red centres of the flowers accentuate the triangle; the green of the centre flower is recalled on the white flower, and the dark purple also on the flower on the left. So also the white of the right-hand flower is carried over on the left; the green bud at the base, recalling the green mass at the top, is also excessively valuable, as giving perpendicularity to the composition. It is difficult to imagine a more exquisite instance of order enlivened by caprice, than in the present example.

The border on the lower portion of the plate is one of those odd compositions so constantly met with, and which would appear to have a meaning, but which is difficult for the European mind to seize. The centre portion is evidently intended to represent a face; the eyes, nose, and mouth can be deciphered.

PLATE LXV.

Another example from a painted china Bottle, of
pure Chinese composition.

PLATE LXVII.

Another of the same class, painted china.

Plate LXXI.

From a painted china Jar. The principle of composition on this bottle is the same as on Plates LXX. and XLVI., only the continuous line runs horizontally instead of spirally round the bottle, and the repeat is moved one-half a division, so as to bring the flowers into triangles. To compose a pattern which shall do this, and thoroughly and evenly fill up the space, is not easy, and is only attained by the Oriental instinct.

PLATE LXXV.

From a painted china Bottle.   This composition
is in the mixed style.   The main stems are continuous, and embrace all the flowers ; but there are distributed over the surface detached emblems, unconnected with the composition.

PLATE LXXVI.

From a painted china Vase.   A composition on
the continuous-stem principle.

Plate LXXVII.

From a painted china Bottle.   A composition
in the fragmentary style. Pure Chinese in character.

PLATE LXXXII.

From a painted china Vase. A very fine example of detached or fragmentary ornamentation.

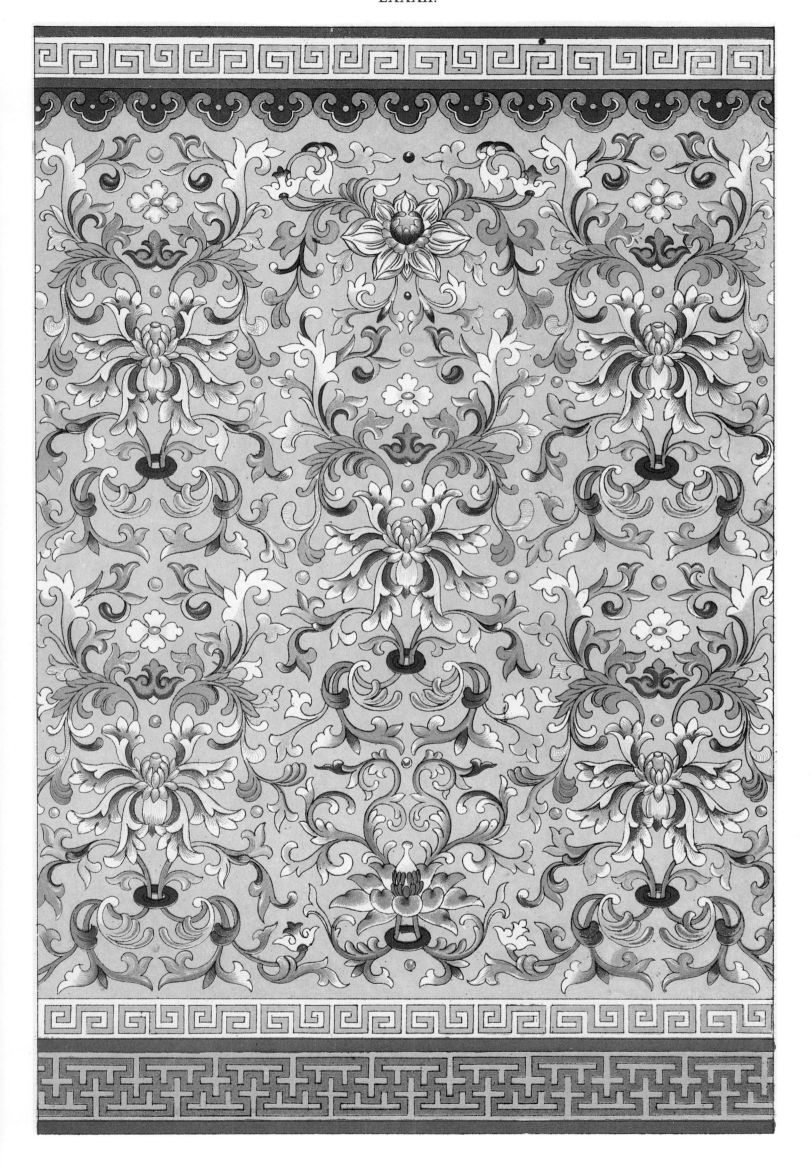

PLATE LXXXIII.

From a painted china Vase. Similar style to the last, but more perfect; in the balance of the masses, the embossed ground is formed of a continuous line of volutes.

Plate LXXXV.

From painted china. The upper example is from
a Basin; the lower is from a portion of a Vase.

PLATE XCII.

From a painted china Vase. A bold composition
on the continuous-stem principle.

PLATE XCV.

From a painted china Vase. Another composition on the fragmentary principle.

Plate XCVI.

From a painted china Bottle. A singular composition; remarkable for the way in which the effect of the strong colour of the ornament is softened by the judicious treatment of the ground.

Plate XCVIII.

Inlaid bronze Dish.